perimeters

perimeters

by

charles levendosky

wesleyan university press

middletown, connecticut

Copyright © 1970 by Charles Levendosky

Hardbound: SBN 8195 1049 1   Paperback: SBN 8195 2049 7

Library of Congress catalog card number: 78–105508

Manufactured in the United States of America

First edition

for love
to charlotte

perimeters

these words

thin ice paving
a raging river

thin ice balances
precariously on air
and those momentary surging swells
that sweep it silently
then rush away

thin ice cracks
parts
and bellies up
under a mans passionate weight

chunks swirl in eddies
dip perpendicular
dive to the muddy bottom
bearing the stain
when they reappear

but i
behind these blooded eyes
pulsing to tell
what a frozen tongue cannot
how do i pour the river
into your lap

jersey turnpike

scrap smoldering
oil puddle vapors
with sludge rings
powerlines crossing themselves
in a haze of wire

          i drive the seattle express to philly
          twice a day
          eat a bite   rest an hour
          & drive the new york express home
          eight hours aday on the bucket
          four days aweek
          been on this route a year

```
        o o o o o o    o o o o o o    o o o o o o
        o                o       o    o
        o o o o          o       o    o       o o o
        o                o       o    o         o
        o                o o o o o o  o o o o o o

o o o o o o  o o o o o o  o o o o      o       o    o o o o o o  o o o o o o
o       o    o            o     o      o       o    o      o     o
o o o o o o  o o o o      o        o        o       o      o     o o o o
o     o      o            o     o      o       o    o      o     o
o     o      o o o o o o  o o o o         o o o o o o  o o o o o o  o o o o o o

    o o o o o o  o o o o o o  o o o o o o  o o o o o o  o o o o
    o            o       o    o            o           o     o
      o o o      o o o o o o  o o o o      o o o o      o       o
        o        o            o            o           o       o
    o o o o o o  o            o o o o o o  o o o o o o  o o o o
```

tenth & linden

camden new jersey
three blocks
of brownstones
a few blacks
relaxing on a porch
drinking beer
watching traffic
cross the bridge to philly
flick
a burning cigarette butt
onto the highway
laughing

       im not gonna show
       no mercy what-so-ever
       for every lick i got
       im gonna give two

      in the idleness
      of words
      where do these stand
      that free a man
      from his burden
      for awhile

the second story bay
hard
brown
most the panes broken

WELCOME
TO
PHILADELPHIA

sure we got subways here
you think new york is the only city
an we got buses and a mayor too

she has the sense
the proportion
smiling woman
on old bowed legs
that cant cross the honking traffic
soon enough

pennsylvania turnpike didactic

out there
always another horizon
not so hidden
beyond the first

you know why its so green
dontcha
this is the first time
i been on this turnpike
when it wasnt rainin
and ive traveled this road
plenny

BLUE MOUNTAIN
          your tax dollars
          are not
          building this tunnel
          tolls are
KITTATINNY MOUNTAIN
          remove
          sunglasses
TUSCARORA MOUNTAIN
          do
          not
          pass   [this little town was
SIDELING HILL   evacuated last night
          end   after a truck-tanker
          65   loaded with explosive
          begin   chemicals sprang a
          50   leak on the busy penn
                    one   turnpike
                    lane   authorities fearful
                    only   of an explosion . . . . .]

                         end
                         50
                         begin
                         35
                                   left
                                   lane
                                   only

RAYS HILL
          falling
          rock
          zone
                    yeah it was named
                    after the foreman who

                    was buried in a cave-in
                    they dug him out
                    only to rebury him
                    on the hill
   ALLEGHENY MOUNTAIN
                    during the rob-barron days
                    when makin money was as spectacular
                    as gunshoots in the west
                    ole cornelius vanderbuilt planned
                    these tunnels for a railroad
                    in a bid for more big money

aluminum refrigerated trailers
with steel cabs
slide by
horsedrawn hayricks
the men of each
brawny in their T shirts
in full control
not a nod is passed

                         [item one (right)
                          two tow trucks
                          fish torn metal
                          from a deep ditch]

truckstop   [item two (left)
                          a hardtop convertible
whatcha doin   flipped on its shell
tomorrow night   a wheel still spins]
             nothin
             say you remembered
             its my night off
sure
i remember things

like that
>   thats what i like
>   high class men
>   gives a woman
>   a sense of security

south of chicago

suckin up taters for dollar an hour
they
threw me outta kankakee
drunk
judge hauled me up
two hundred dollar fine
or forty days in jail
at five dollars a day
didnt have the money

okey he said
get outta illinois

>   turned his back
>   to the wind
>   so the tabacco
>   wouldnt blow
>   from the trough
>   of paper
>   between two fingers
>   rollin his own
>   a lick along the edge
>   & a twist at each end

the boss owed me twentyfive dollars
for three days work
said he didnt owe me nothin
but hed give me five
outta kindness
had to borrow ten more
to buy the bus ticket
to tupelo
the sheriff at my shoulder
watchin
closest to mobile
i could get
never been there
hope they got crop work

grain elevators
rise
broad white
above narrow roads

      a town marker
      that bends the road
      to the right

**WELCOME
TO
BELLFLOWER!**
Pop 650
Buy Sharwheat
ITS THE BEST!

farmer city journal

silo
butler units
corncribs
soybeans & corn
population 1700
church
short double-breath mainstreet
package goods store for liquor & beer
soda-drug store
feed & grain shack
supermarket
church
come again (rotary club)
soybean & corn
corncribs
butler units
drive-in theater

chicago diary

earth
flat as if to mock
the lake
show it how
it should be
&
sliced
for uneven
distribution

a city
with rural voices
continually
reminded of nature
by corn & wheat
lake & river

    seeker of lower levels
    font of life

keeps the buildings low
and movement horizontal

      hell
      its the wind
      that makes em
      afraid of height

        it still
        blows the earth & sky
        around
        if aint somethin
        holdin em down

wooden fire-scapes
slap painted
ship-yard gray
leaning
against brick walls
nailed for support

and the flophouse
        second-hand shop
        cheap tavern
section

CHICAGO TRIB

you dont know how bad it is
here on the street
these men are victims of jackrollers
everynight
and theyre beaten
            kicked
            & even killed
for the change in their pockets
and no one cares

            what makes us
            jackup a wino
            for half a buck
            or
            curse & chase
            a man who eats
            from garbage bins
            wolf
            &
            prey
            ourselves

and the ratio of energy expended to calculable gains
computed in steps /¢

      you cant sit long
      at a booth with only
      a cup of coffee
      sir

chicago waiting room (in & out)

breasts hanging
pulling a black sweater
down
to black toreador pants
where the flesh folds twice
tightly
    a heavy maltese cross
    pendant
            pendulous
reading a pulp
action book
CYCLE FURY
holding it with her tatooed hand

      born
       to
      lose

jerks a pen
& notebook
from the pocket

of her slouching man
       hey wake up
       you gotta be tough
       to be in a cycle gang
thickly fingering
the small pages
before writing
       theres something more
       you gotta get besides
       my white bridalgown

redcap

its always good to get home
i always say
always glad to get away
and gladder still to get home

yes mam

minneapolis directory

used to be called flour-city
in fact youll see old signs
saying
      FLOUR CITY   **HOME OF GENERAL MILLS**

                    star of the north
                    city of lakes
                    grain city
                    milling capital of the world
                    home of pillsbury & general mills

minneapolis grain exchange
buckle on the grain belt
great northern railroad spreading the wheat

movement
of freight
    truck & auto
sluicing
through great carved canals
depressed & compressed earth
carries the burden
of our wants

                    nicollet avenue
                    shopping district of minneapolis
                    the fifth avenue of the west

westward

used to drive
a tractor
three or four years ago
cant now
nor a combine either
complicated machinery

it changes each year
my dad bought
some new contrivances
this year
only spends his money
on farm machines
hes tight with it
otherwise

> cant talk to him
> about this time ayear
> while you pay 30¢
> for a loaf of bread
> the farmers gettin
> $1.25 a bushel wheat
> hes touchy about it
> gets sore easy

nothin much in
north dakota
you seen five minutes
of it
you seen it all
a few cottonwood trees
on riverbottoms
or where folks
planted them
> wheat flat
> cept the southwestern end
> rollin to the badlands
wheat is what we grow
or
broomgrass & sweetclover
when the government pays us

not to plant
    cant even cut it
    for cattle feed
    the government owns it

my father made money
on coal
found it on his land
strip mining half his acreage
bettern wheat
anyday
even if it peels the soil away

been to school
in minneapolis
comin home
dont like the city
worked three weeks for a family
at eight dollars aweek
and room & board
so i could make
a little money
and live near the school
but i quit
work you like a horse
they advertize in the papers

      farm girl wanted to help
      with family chores . . .

i guess they figure
theyll get a good
dumb girl

who ll work hard
for little money

    i guess it works
    alright

montana views

highway
stitching with the great northern rails
a cloth
of cut hay
bailed
laying to be shipped
leaving
a tan tweed stubble

a town
of twohundred
and on a hill
between farms
a small barbfenced
graveyard
with white wooden markers
and a shed
for shovels & rope

continental divide
pine
fir
and caught
tumbling rock

        continental divide
        splays the flow
        into east & west

WELCOME TO BUTTE
Richest Hill On Earth
Pop 46454   El 5715ft

butte
built on a hill
once & still
the highest mile on earth
runs down a slope
shacks & bars at the bottom
precarious mainstreet
slipping
rud brick buildings
with horseshoe arch windows
slide down
to wood

STRIKE

when the copper mines
shut down
its the men
have stopped

wanting meager profits
from the tonnage
they move

which moves
by four rails
four winds
to the mills

& silver into the pockets
of the few
they will never know

[see the statue   [a butte man
of marus daly   secured
founder of   electric blasting caps
the anaconda co   around his throat and
and one of   above his ears
the copper kings   then
of buttes   threatened
colorful early days]   to plug himself in]

idaho (point & vector)

on the side
of a bare
rain eroded
mountain
spelled in white
boulders

KEEP   IDAHO

GREEN

a winding
stream
looping
with the highway
chalk-gray
by copper mine
leaching

provo sighting

in utah
a local night bus
veered
to a gravel ledge
braked
the driver leapt
into the bright
uncanny light

      i thought it was
      the end
      the sky all aglow
      i wanted to smell the sage
      and bitter mountain grass
      one last time

the backpage
of a salt lake daily
carried the story
the following day
of a meteorite
of unusual size & brilliance
passing overhead

spokane pause

a punched down
straw stetson
coveralls
foot on the rail
and a mug of cold beer

      its the only thing
      to do
      in heat like this

seattle diary

00
1st Ave
and at one end
FRONTIER PARK
a triangle of trees
a totem
(built under the supervision
of the department of parks)
& lunging sprawling drunks
no number for it
whores in bars
peddlers & panhandlers
shuffling the drab
lower streets

pawnshops
prostitutes
& bars
alternate to strip
a man bare

see
those were fourteen dollar shoes
you know
think he gave me a buck for them
hell no
half
fifty cents
now hows a man
supposed to tank up on that

                say
                can you
                help a man out

crowds
watching a steel ball
swing
bounce & batter
concrete into chunks

                thats the old orpheum theater

wondering
at the quantity
of steel
that webs
the crumbling stone

                they made real buildings in those days

at the way
the crushed walls
lean
in shreds
but do not fall

hoping
the edifice
will win

                gonna put a hotel up there
                i hear
                dont know why we let these money people
                in here
                to tear down our buildings

down the coast

when i first came here
from germany
and had traveled along
the columbia river
i wrote back
            its just like the rhine
            but without castles
            or barges
you know
ive been here fiftyfour years
its my home now

            newberg/oregon

            must have been hot
            last night
            four mattresses on the lawn
            & three sleeping
            children
            one boy
            in bathing trunks
            already playing

she took
her perogative
as an old woman
to prod everyone
into childhood

but lightly
with humor
      i saw the breakfast
      you ate
      (clicking her tongue & shaking her head)
      donuts
      were they good

redwood
from the road
a barren hilltop
seems scattered
with toothpicks

      redwood
      a truck
      can move
      only a section
      of one
      at a time

truckers & busdrivers
comrades
of the road
honk or wave
at each other
going opposite
directions

             after a few years
             on a route
             a man gets to recognize
             other regulars
known by
a route
         a wave
                   & a machine

real dry this year
aint like it used to be
a friend of mine
took me for a drive
in the mountains
and said
             watch for smog
and by god
there it was
hangin low
circling the mountain
like a ring of cigar smoke
all from one papermill

from one little pulp & paper mill

stinkin up the air
americans
we aint never done nothing right
spoil everything we touch
since the first settlers
moved west

you watch the hills
from reedsport to coosbay
been barren of trees
for fifty to sixty years
they plant one for each one cut
they say
but they dont

why they cut down
six or eight small trees
(indicating girth by bowed hands—tips to tips)
to pull a felled one
(indicating a girth three times as great)
to the truck
an a government man
supervising them
when with a chain
to the truck they coulda
snaked it between them young ones

reedsport frame

jobs in
lumber & plywood mills
each box house
has a chimney
& in the small square yard
a pile of wood chips

      managers
      halfway down & round
      the hill
      smogless
      for the view from picture windows
      of uncut fir & pine
      & their own church

coosbay frame

lumber stacked
& banded
on the docks
      timber piled
      high & wide
      sprayed with river water
      or corralled in it
      a floating floor

PEELER LOGS WANTED

bandon to bookings

fog
blows cold
from the ocean
held
impaled on pines

road ethics

look at that guy
he knows we want to pass
yet he speeds up
       wait until we re goin
       downhill
       we ll catch up
       then
       give him a blast
       of that horn

you got a jug there
lady
       you can check it
       with your luggage
but you cant
have it on board

the descent of a voice
too slowly

san francisco diary

waves
rolling over
sliding down
hills
submerge streets
lamps & houses
in fog
a radio tower
peaks above
yes
there is a city
beneath

saw a man shot right on that corner
first time i was here

across the street
from the bus depot
at three
in the morning
talking to another
in the trade
& remaking her face
at the table
of a 24hour cafeteria
its a callus business
and lonely

alright what kinda thing
ya want to do

i do ya anything at thirty dollars
for half an hour

prevent runaways
turn wheel into curb
set brake
park in gear

when i saw these hills
i didnt think any car could make it

south of frisco

migrant workers
wind
bending
windbreaks
men
bending
to pick the soil
of its fruit

their gray box
huts
stand hot
ovens
in the sun

tomato crates
potato sacks
& green pea combines
we eat by your labor

halcyon road
a wave of birds
dots the sea
while
the sun hunters
of pismo beach
dine

foothills
worn smooth
brown
as if the shrubbery
had been rubbed off
hurriedly
leaving hints of green
in the folds & valleys

coastline south (soliloquy)

fortyfive years shipbuilding
workin machinery
prided myself for keepin
all my fingers
                then i went
and dropped a wrench
reached over to grab it
got my hand caught
in a belt
                whipped into the machinery
took my fingernail off
& chipped the bone at the top

                    fishin off moro bay
                    barely caught enough
                    to pay
                    ton & ahalf   albacor & tuna
                    usually catch twelve to thirteen tons

bought fourteen hundred
dollars worth of equipment
and it didnt last one day
sure
theres a guarantee alright
but
what good does that do you
out there
a hundred miles from shore

                    while she was livin
                    i never went fishin
                    i d never be runnin now
                    im too old for it
                     anymore

children tried to talk me
into marrying again
but i dont want to have
a woman go through
what i went through
when i lost her
and i dont want
to go through it again

LA dialogue

spider city
lacing your asphalt web
over sourthern california
do you trap so many
that the air
singes with your poison

        beverly hills
        islands of leaves
        soil on the sidewalks

            strolled twelve blocks
            at ten this morning
            without meeting anyone
            suddenly realized
            the crowds
            were in the streets
            driving

      stucco & palm
      spread low
      brown hills beyond

mechanized
newspaper vendors
put a dime in the slot

**PULL DOOR UP AND OUT
REMOVE   NEWSPAPER**

they dont talk back
with greed laden voices
but you cant argue
when they short-change you

supermarkets & freeways
im tired of los angeles
lets go on a vacation

el centro   111 miles

el centro by three
but el cajon was first
and a road
through usedcar valley
valley ends
onestory false adobes end

khaki earth creased
by concrete ducts
tanned weeds erect
along the asphalt trail
DEVILS HIGHWAY

up
boulder studded barehills
that tolerate oak
not scrub
but almost
green trees
ash with dust
even through the tintedglass
mobilehomes not mobile
        aluminum coffins
          reflecting sunpoints hotly
occasional cactus grows
among the weathered rock
outnumbered

HIGHWAY ENDS ½ MILE

where paintscraped earthmovers
shove foothills into beds
for asphalt planes
        and
        plains

CALEXICO EXIT 1 MILE

where mountains
have been ironed flat
by sunpowered
airless winds
        datepalm
        cotton bolls
        nutpalm
on this brutish anvil
ringing with heat

where mountains are
        hopes
        dreams
        mirages
and houses are
        rectangular
        brown
        sentryboxes
on grassless earth
seeming
always
to need repair
even when new

EL CENTRO CITY LIMITS

yuma rest stop

sand sage & tumbleweed
odor
of hot dust
percolated
by the sun

tanned hide
relief map
of canyon
of arroyo
where one lives
molds ones face
and casts the pallor

he always talked about
the dunes as if they were
naked pregnant women
called those wind ripples
stretch marks
they been waiting a long time
to birth
unless the reptiles are theirs

SOFT
SHOULDER
SAND

4:30 / 110°
by the rotating sign
on a local bank
yet on a bench
in the sun
on old indian woman
in a wide loose red cotton print dress

and a black cotton shawl
selling
felt & bead craft

travelers turn their watches forward
one hour upon arriving
heading east

gila bend to phoenix

prickly pear
staghorn cactus
& a foothill background

DONT BE A BOLLWORM RANCHER
KILL EM

palo verde
blooms
bright yellow
they tell you
now
a leafless
green stick

phoenix to flagstaff

tales told by titles

       black canyon city

       bloody basin road

       horse thief basin

flagstaff
at night
cool
the smell of pine
& the warning blast
of a santa fe train

gallup & eastward

bus depot playhouse
two indians
sweat & rain soiled
straw stetsons
above eyes
quick with laughter
nudging each other

       they come in here
       every evening
       sit for hours
       watching the passengers

albuquerque to santa fe

on a circle
of earth
rimmed by
a cloverleaf freeway exit
a cemetary
of stones & crosses

santa fe (the development of a city)

arroyos couldnt be built in
so people built alongside them
they came to be used as streets
rich & poor alike walk on dirt

       its the sky
       that one notices here
       the dominant fugue
       clouds above mountains
       variation on a theme

adobe
wood   clay & straw
sunbaked pink
on the mesas

bus talk

my ex-husband
telephoned me last night
said for me to get-on back
heard i been runnin around
i told him he d better
send some money
if he wanted to see me
cant get rid of him
no matter where i go
he finds me
he wired the money to the busdepot
just the amount for the ticket
wait til i see him
what about cigarette money
i ll tell him

terminal (for two voices)

from
california to oklahoma
gray dungarees
gray workshirt
clad bus rider
as if from town to farm
homecut whitehair swirling
from the vortex
where the headrests

sixty-yeared hands
hard
wide as long
(like shaking hands
 with pineknots)
stuck into dark
of pockets
hooded
while he ambles
to loosen
seatstiff leg muscles
USED TO WALKIN
NOT SETTIN
a tongue
of handkerchief
hangs lapping red
from his walletpocket

sixty-yeared hands
veins reliefed
like root-ridges
that grip
soil banks
converge to
earthcrusted
nails
and
scar callused
finger stubs
that jut from
his fists
taproots
wretched
wrenched loose
of nature

oklahoma city (wind & speeches)

rich in oil
rich in history
"an that aint all"
oil
on the capitol lawn
the easy squeek
& chug of pumps
# OIL CAPITOL OF THE WORLD
oklahoma
an old choctaw name
with "plenny of tales
tied to it"

we have our greats
& we had em
why the whole world
knew of will rogers
and who aint heard of
oklahoma football

eighty-two years old
before i spent a day
in a hospital
& that on account of
a car accident
broke my collarbone
ah its all knit up
fine now
just a little lump
doctor said i d
probably live to be
a hundred

came here in the sooner rush
worked a homestead
with my husband
til the dustbowl days
then moved to the city

sold my car
when i turned seventyfive
could drive today
as good as ever
if folks just stay
outta my way

indications

"boy
this is my kinna weather"

red clay
rolling ozarks
live oak
and diseased elm

CLABBER GIRL

more pickup trucks
than
autos

ROY "BUDDY" McTEASLY
FOR   REPRESENTATIVE

° ponca city

                       O tulsa

         ° sapulpa

     ° bristow   ° tahlequah

    °shawnee

light blue fords
on the roads
in the heaps
dominating hue
blends with the sky
not so much protective coloring
as resonance
with the dominant theme

tulsa depot entry

negro drunk
slumped out
flat
clutching a union
picket sign

    the patrolman
    who gathered him up
    & led him to the car
    later returned to pick up
    the black battered lunchpail

fort smith depot entry

    "niggas
     they just yellin
     they just yellin"
as they load

and clean the buses
earning to get their tickets
out

      "hey boy
       how come my bus aint
       loaded yet"

"ticket PLEASE"
black woman
diggin down
the front of her dress
to fish out
a worn change purse
the color of her skin
"ticket NORTH"

ozarks

my husband and i
go to fort smith
airport
watch them planes
come in
boy
i tell you
they got some big ones

      yeah neighbor
      we got deer

see some everyday
round my house
some ole boys
huntin some the other day
said theys real good

slight
& bowed
to fit his hands
in the overalls
speaks in low tones
of a whisper
looking at the ground

little rock to memphis (sunday)

from brick homes
with shaded lawns
to cotton gins
          sharecroppers
                    & their leaning churches
stuck into red clay earth
even the six lane highway
narrows to a thin single road
snaking
between cotton crops
express becomes local
stops for a preacher
shuttling through his parish
& he forced to listen

(as he must have many times before)
with mild humor
& taut dark dignity
to an aged town athiest
chide him about
            "baptists think theyre
                the onliest ones goin to heaven"

they arrive
in cars
or by foot
some following
the well hoed rows
to an odd&ends shanty
smaller than a barn
not as well pieced together

they gather
what they can
of themselves
to wait
the word of god

memphis then northward

memphis downtown
evacuated by whites

            [this bluff was fortified by
            general pillow may 1862]

conscious of dates
of time past
even a street
named
                [november 6th 1934]

is there a memory
hidden
in some rotting corner
a memory
of those buffalo soldiers
of the civil war
who had surrendered at fort pillow
who were shot
hands and feet tied in a belly-down arc

raleigh (center of gravity)

history
stalks two blocks south
of hillsborough street
markers
at every intersection
there
one recalls
who
ran the raleigh tribune
in 1852

a church steeple
is tallest
in old raleigh
adjacent to
a redbrick gothic mansion
in fading black trimming
a funeral wreath
fallen
upright
between door & screening

raleigh (perimeters)

arc beds
timber struts
& galvanized iron walls
    engine stalls empty
    tracks sinking into creosote & soil
    & the smell of the ironhorse
        lingers
        droppings not yet dry
        in the silence of our decay
the turntable
rooted to rust
pit
track
& shack immobile
the motor gone
    scraps
    & some iron wheels
    frozen in place

but

others roll
wheel against rail
steel on steel
a sound that grits the teeth
in its grinding solidness

> "whats left moves
> anyway"

L A B O R
PICK-UP ZONE
½ block south

been comin here
every day
for fifteen years
at four in the mornin
hoping for work at good pay
folks that stop here
want cheap labor
man pulled up yesterday

> want ten men to gravel
> a road
> i can only pay a dollar
> en a quarter an hour

thats the usual wage
aint much
but it keeps a man an his family
in beans and rags

an open market square
surrounding a warehouse
at breezeless noon
local produce
of melons & yams
        a squat woman grinning
        a gold tooth
        as she weighs
        the choice
        on a handscale

THE CAPITOL

sunup
a thin hunched man
walks
from a bus stop
to the treasury building
carrying his lunch
in a brownpaper sack

        sandwiched
        between
                the white house
                and the court house
        burlesque
        girlie flicks
        & streetwalkers

        the meat between
        thin white bread

a woman in a window
dark in her slip
smoking a cigarette
shakes her head
no
"ive had a long night honey"

the greyhound narrator

this is your thru
nonstop
greyhound coach
to new york
        that thriving metropolis
it makes the trip
from wondorous washington dc
in four hours ten minutes
. . . .
baltimore has perhaps
the largest number of
ROWHOUSES
houses which share a common wall
rich & poor alike live in them
& the porches are spotlessly clean
most being scrubbed every day
. . . .
the next point of interest
just ahead
is the delaware memorial bridge
which connects
delaware and new jersey
you will see another span
being erected

**NO   STOPPING
ON
BRIDGE AHEAD**

while crossing
the delaware river today
is only a matter
of getting to the other side
picture in your minds eye
the historic significance
of general washingtons crossing
some twohundred years ago

movement & suspension

catenary
the fall of cable
from two points
(not on a vertical)
pulled
from its curve
to parabola
by load after load
of bridging
  catenary
  the fall of cable
  from two points
  anchor post to anchor post
  piling to piling
  the easy swing
  set into motion
  by salt wind & pulsing gusts

[j.f. hager   chief engineer
died in a fall from an insecure
cantilevered   section]

parabola
the arc
a man makes
from birth to death
from pinnacle to pinnacle
of trauma
supported by the catenary
of his will
            his life the load
            the bridging
            from here to there

            footbridge
            drawbridge
            pontoon
            bascule
            panel-truss
buffeted into oscillation
set into the resonance
of their destruction
crack & plunge riverward
some sooner
            some later
all these temporary spans

Distinguished contemporary poetry in cloth and paperback editions

ALAN ANSEN: *Disorderly Houses* (1961)

JOHN ASHBERY: *The Tennis Court Oath* (1962)

ROBERT BAGG: *Madonna of the Cello* (1961)

MICHAEL BENEDIKT: *The Body* (1968)

ROBERT BLY: *Silence in the Snowy Fields* (1962)

GRAY BURR: *A Choice of Attitudes* (1969)

TURNER CASSITY: *Watchboy, What of the Night?* (1966)

TRAM COMBS: *saint thomas. poems.* (1965)

DONALD DAVIE: *Events and Wisdoms* (1965); *New and Selected Poems* (1961)

JAMES DICKEY: *Buckdancer's Choice* (1965) [National Book Award in Poetry, 1966]; *Drowning With Others* (1962); *Helmets* (1964)

DAVID FERRY: *On the Way to the Island* (1960)

ROBERT FRANCIS: *The Orb Weaver* (1960)

JOHN HAINES: *Winter News* (1966)

EDWIN HONIG: *Spring Journal: Poems* (1968)

RICHARD HOWARD: *The Damages* (1967); *Quantities* (1962)

BARBARA HOWES: *Light and Dark* (1959)

DAVID IGNATOW: *Figures of the Human* (1964); *Rescue the Dead* (1968); *Say Pardon* (1961)

DONALD JUSTICE: *Night Light* (1967); *The Summer Anniversaries* (1960) [A Lamont Poetry Selection]

CHESTER KALLMAN: *Absent and Present* (1963)

PHILIP LEVINE: *Not This Pig* (1968)

LOU LIPSITZ: *Cold Water* (1967)

JOSEPHINE MILES: *Kinds of Affection* (1967)

VASSAR MILLER: *My Bones Being Wiser* (1963); *Onions and Roses* (1968); *Wage War on Silence* (1960)

W. R. MOSES: *Identities* (1965)

LEONARD NATHAN: *The Day the Perfect Speakers Left* (1969)

DONALD PETERSEN: *The Spectral Boy* (1964)

MARGE PIERCY: *Breaking Camp* (1968)

HYAM PLUTZIK: *Apples from Shinar* (1959)

VERN RUTSALA: *The Window* (1964)

HARVEY SHAPIRO: *Battle Report* (1966)

JON SILKIN: *Poems New and Selected* (1966)

LOUIS SIMPSON: *At the End of the Open Road* (1963) [Pulitzer Prize in Poetry, 1964]; *A Dream of Governors* (1959)

JAMES WRIGHT: *The Branch Will Not Break* (1963); *Saint Judas* (1959); *Shall We Gather at the River* (1968)